MURRAY AVE. LIBRARY
LOWER MORELAND SCH. DIST.
HUNTINGDON VLY, PA.

HOW THEY LIVED

AN AMERICAN PIONEER FAMILY

ROBIN MAY

Illustrated by
Mark Bergin

ROURKE ENTERPRISES, INC.
Vero Beach, Florida 32964

First published in the
United States in 1987 by
Rourke Enterprises, Inc.
PO Box 3328, Vero Beach,
Florida 32964

First Published in 1985 by
Wayland (Publishers) Limited
61 Western Road, Hove
East Sussex BN3 1JD, England

© Copyright 1985 Wayland (Publishers) Limited

Typeset by Kalligraphics Ltd, Redhill, Surrey.
Printed in Italy by G. Canale & C.S.p.A., Turin

All rights reserved. No part of this book may be reproduced or utilized
in any form or by any means electronic or mechanical including photocopying,
recording or by any information storage
and retrieval system without permission in writing from the publishers.

Library of Congress Cataloging-in-Publication Data

May, Robin.
An American pioneer family.

(How they lived)
Bibliography: p.
Includes index.
Summary: Surveys the daily life of pioneer families in the American West, describing their travel, homes, clothing, food and drink, health, education, religion, recreation, and relationships with each other.
1. Frontier and pioneer life — West (U.S.) — Juvenile literature. 2. Pioneers — West (U.S.) — Juvenile literature. 3. West (U.S.) — Social life and customs — Juvenile literature. [1. Frontier and pioneer life. 2. West (U.S.) — Social life and customs] I. Bergin, Mark, ill. II. Title. III. Series: How they lived (Vero Beach, Fla.)
F596.M345   1987   978   86-20234
ISBN 0-86592-138-5

Contents

A LONG, HARD JOURNEY   4

THE COVERED WAGON   6

BUILDING A HOME   8

FAMILY LIFE   10

WHAT PIONEERS WORE   12

FOOD AND DRINK   14

HEALTH AND SICKNESS   16

GOING TO SCHOOL   18

FACING DANGERS   20

A TRIP TO TOWN   22

RELIGION   24

RECREATION   26

CRIME AND PUNISHMENT   28

THE END OF THE FRONTIER   30

GLOSSARY   31

INDEX   32

A Long, Hard Journey

They were nearing their journey's end. Everyone was walking beside the covered wagons that were inching their way along a dangerous part of the trail through the Rocky Mountains. There was a gorge on one side and a fast flowing river far below on the other. A swerve to the right or left would have ended in disaster.

These pioneers, and others like them, made history. They had braved marauding Indians, dust storms, and extremes of heat and cold on their 1,800-mile (3,000-kilometer) crossing of North America, from Independence, Missouri, to the "promised land" of Oregon, on the Pacific coast.

As they made their way west, the pioneers crossed an area known as the Great American Desert. It was a vast, treeless region. People

The Oregon and California Trails

The route to the West took the brave pioneers across the Great American Desert and over the Rocky Mountains.

thought crops would not grow there. It stretched from the Missouri River to the Rocky Mountains and from Texas to the Canadian border. In the 1860s and after, however, a new wave of pioneers swarmed onto this land, renamed the plains, which was found very suitable for farming. This book will tell you about the people who made the new lands their home.

THE COVERED WAGON

There was nothing fancy about a covered wagon. It was usually a converted farm wagon. There were some wagons, called prairie schooners, which were built for long journeys. Most of these big wagons were used for trading.

The covered wagon was home for the pioneers on their long trip west. They packed as much as they could into them – tools for farming and building, cooking utensils, bedding, weapons, food, water and a few luxuries like furniture. Some things were tied to the sides of the wagon. Wagons were usually pulled by oxen. On a long journey the animals grew weak. Many things had to be discarded to lighten their load.

Wagon trains were often led across the plains by a guide.

A pioneer family and their covered wagon "home".

Inside the covered wagon was a bed like a wooden box. It was 13 feet (4 meters) long and about 3 feet (one meter) wide. The whole family slept here. Usually the wagon's canvas cover was kept up as protection against dust and rain, but in very hot weather it was folded back.

Wagons had no springs. They often lost a wheel or broke apart and many families never finished the journey. On the trails to Oregon and California, it was vital for pioneers to get to their destination before the winter snows blocked the mountain passes. When the long journey came to an end, each family settled on a chosen spot. Wagons that had survived were again used for farm work.

Sometimes the wagon trains were attacked by bands of Indians.

BUILDING A HOME

In the northwest, with its great forests, homes were built of wood. But on the plains to the east and south there were hardly any trees at all. So the first homes that many pioneers built on the plains were made by digging into a mound or hill. This formed a single cave-like room called a dugout. Dugouts were dirty and unhealthy and were only temporary homes.

Next came a sod house. Pioneers who built with sod – the earth – became known as sodbusters. The sodbusting age can be said to date from 1862 when the government gave 160 acres to anyone who wanted them for a small fee.

To build a sod house the sod was cut into blocks three feet (one meter) long. These blocks were used in much the same way as we use bricks today. Spaces were left for windows and a door. Rafters, to support the roof, were made of brushwood. Only families with money could afford a framed timber roof. The roof was made of a layer of prairie grass covered with sod. The spaces between the sod were filled with soil. Doors and windows were covered with buffalo skins or blankets to keep out drafts. A length of pipe through the roof served as a chimney.

Sod houses were not much healthier than dugouts. It was difficult to keep them dry inside in heavy rain but at least they were cool during the hot summers and warm in the freezing winters. Because the walls were made of earth, sod houses were also safe from fire.

Sod houses were built from blocks of earth cut out of the ground.

Early pioneers on the plains made their homes in dugouts **(above left)**. *In the northwest, log cabins were more common* **(above right)**.

FAMILY LIFE

A pioneer family needed strength and courage to survive. Pioneers had to grow their own food. Corn, or maize, was the main crop. There were no machines to help them farm, and the ground was very hard. Some pioneers had to use axes to break the soil. Oxen or horses were used for jobs like plowing. The whole family helped: the men did the plowing and other heavy work; the wives tended a vegetable garden; and the children milked the cows, fed the animals and collected chickens' eggs.

Pioneer families were often lonely. The nearest neighbor might be 30 miles (50 kilometers) away. Many things had to be faced alone. One wife recalled fighting bedbugs and flies all summer and scrubbing floors to keep her house clean. Water had to be pumped out of the well by hand. Many wives died young and many children died too. Despite this, families were usually large.

On the plains, buffalo droppings were collected for fuel.

A large pioneer family seated in front of their sod house.

A pioneer's wife rarely had time to leave the farm, there was always work to be done. She had to make all the family's clothes, cook the meals, clean the house, bake bread and grow vegetables as well as help on the farm. Her husband occasionally went into town or visited another farm. A trip to the nearest town was usually made to buy supplies like salt, coffee, flour and seeds for next year's crops. For the pioneer family, life was mostly work and very little play.

WHAT PIONEERS WORE

From the picture on this page you can see the sort of clothes a pioneer family wore. They brought their eastern clothes with them when they came West, but these soon wore out. Then the women had to make new clothes for their families.

Pioneers' clothes were usually homemade and heavily patched. Women and children often went barefoot.

Men wore trousers of denim or duck. Both these fabrics are made from cotton and are very hard wearing. Washing and the hot sun soon faded colored garments. Clothes looked even more faded when a bright, new patch was sewn onto them. In the winter, some pioneers dressed like trappers in animal skins. Clothes were worn until they could no longer be patched or mended. Men usually had just one pair of trousers. If they needed repairing, the husband went to bed while his wife got out her sewing basket.

Women wore long dresses made from calico, another type of cotton.

Pioneer women wore long dresses made from calico.

Godey's Lady's Book *helped pioneer women keep up with the fashions.*

Some wore bonnets or shawls around their heads to shade their faces from the burning sun. In towns, pioneers could keep up with fashion. They were helped by a publication called *Godey's Lady's Book*. A poor pioneer wife who liked the look of a silk dress could copy it in cotton.

Shoes were a problem. Many pioneers copied the Indians and wore soft leather moccasins. They bought their boots too big because the leather shrank when it got wet. Most people went barefoot in the summer. In the winter, pioneers wrapped rags around their feet because they had no socks.

Food and Drink

The first pioneer families in the West enjoyed an excellent diet. They could hunt buffalo, deer, turkey, duck and other wild animals. But by the 1870s much of the wildlife had vanished. The more pioneers there were in the West, the more animals were killed to feed them.

The buffalo was almost wiped out because it provided food, leather, and warm coats. Pioneers suffered from its disappearance but not as much as some Indian tribes who depended on the buffalo completely for food, shelter and clothing.

There were still many small animals and birds to be hunted, but gradually the pioneers had to depend more and more on the crops they could grow and the animals they could raise, like pigs and cows.

There were wild fruits and nuts to be gathered. These were usually preserved for the long winter. Sugar was in very short supply, but in the forested areas, a sweet syrup could be extracted from maple trees.

Corn bread was the main type of bread. It was nourishing but tasteless. Children took sandwiches of corn bread and molasses to school. Some families had to eat lard instead of butter, and turnips instead of potatoes.

There were usually two main meals eaten each day and they were rather boring. Here is a typical pioneer family's food for one day:

Breakfast: Corn bread, salt pork and black coffee.
Dinner: Wild greens, boiled pork and cold corn bread washed down with a "beverage" made from vinegar, brown sugar and warm creek water.

The pioneers' main drink was coffee. During and after the Civil War (1861 to 1865) it was very expensive, so coffee was sometimes made with two parts peas to one of coffee.

Early pioneers hunted the buffalo until they were nearly extinct.

HEALTH AND SICKNESS

In the early 1800s, when pioneers were first settling in the West, there were no hospitals and very few nurses. The nearest doctor was often more than thirty miles (fifty kilometers) away. Doctors' bills were expensive for poor pioneers, but sometimes they could pay him with a horse or a cow. Usually, though, it fell to the neighbors to help the sick and people gradually learned which herbs and homemade concoctions could be used to cure illness. They made up all kinds of remedies: coal oil for dandruff; sassafras tea to cure spring fever; well-roasted mouse for measles; and nine shotgun pellets swallowed for boils.

For the pioneers, medical treatment was usually primitive and painful.

Snakes were a hazard. One treatment for a snakebite was to pour turpentine over it and make the victim drink whiskey. This would at least cheer him up and, so it was thought, counteract the effect of the bite.

If surgery was necessary, chloroform was used to put the patient to sleep. A friend or a member of the patient's family had to administer more chloroform to keep him asleep as the doctor operated.

There were outbreaks of killer diseases in the West, like cholera, typhoid, diphtheria and smallpox. Cholera spread very quickly and could kill whole families. Dirty water and poor living conditions often encouraged these diseases.

Gunshot wounds, some accidental and some not, were quite common and medical treatment was usually needed. Many babies were born without the help of a doctor. Neightboring wives gave assistance when they could.

"Quack" doctors, with "miracle cures" for just about everything, often visited towns in the West.

GOING TO SCHOOL

School teachers were famous and very important figures in the West. They were often only a year or two older than their pupils. Teachers usually worked on their own with no one else to help them. It was not easy.

In the early days, teachers often had no house and had to stay with the pupils' families. They went from house to house in turn. When a school was built in the West it was an important event. Parents often paid for the actual building of the school. There were always some people, however, who objected to money being spent on education.

Subjects taught at these schools included history, religion, arithmetic, geography, spelling, agriculture, grammar and reading. Between classes there were playground

The opening of a new school was always a great occasion.

games. Games that needed no equipment, like hide-and-seek, were especially popular. There were always shortages in the classroom. Some schools opened with no books or desks and not even a blackboard.

Pupils who lived on farms outside the town had to travel a long way to get to school. Children in the West were used to hardships and the walk to school was probably quite enjoyable for them.

On the last day of school there was often entertainment for the parents. This was an opportunity for them to see what their children had learned. It might include poetry reading, spelling competitions and a picnic. Prizes were given to children who had worked very hard.

Right *A western schoolteacher listens while some of her class read.*

Below *Children of all ages were taught by one teacher.*

FACING DANGERS

Pioneers were constantly aware of the threat of danger. Most feared were the Indians. Before the pioneers came west the land was inhabited by Indians. Gradually, the white men settled and farmed on Indian land. The result was racial hatred with victory in the end for the far more numerous white settlers.

Because they were badly treated, and promises made by the white man were broken, the Indians fought back. Many innocent pioneers lost their lives for the wrongs of others. Today we rightly see the Indian

A pioneer father returns to find his home destroyed by Indians.

During a range war, pioneers were sometimes killed by wealthy ranchers hungry for their land.

point of view, but we can also understand the feelings of a pioneer father returning home to find his family killed and his farm burned to the ground. The Indian wars were not finally over until the 1890s.

Pioneers had plenty of white enemies too. Ranchers often wanted their land to raise cattle. They sometimes ordered their cowboys to harass sodbusters, even kill them. Women, however, were respected and rarely harmed.

Sometimes full-scale range wars broke out. In 1892, Johnson County, Wyoming, was invaded by 50 Texas gunfighters. They had been hired by local cattle barons to wipe out some of the small ranchers and pioneers in that area. The cattle barons accused them of being rustlers – cattle thieves. The plan didn't work and the gunmen were defeated. After that, settlers and ranchers gradually learned to share the land. Even so, they still had natural hazards to face, like killer diseases, dust storms and plagues of locusts.

A Trip to Town

A trip to the nearest town provided the lonely pioneers with a chance to stock up with provisions and to meet their friends.

Going to town in the West could sometimes mean a trip to a place with several thousand inhabitants. More often it meant a long journey to a handful of wooden shacks set in the middle of a wilderness. Yet what we would call a small village was like an oasis in a desert to a lonely pioneer. In town, there would be a chance to go shopping and to meet people.

Some towns were very tough indeed, with cowboys relaxing after a long cattle drive. They were likely to get drunk and start gunfights unless there were brave lawmen to stop them. It was dangerous for pioneers to be in town at the same time as these troublemakers.

A hardware store and townspeople of Dodge City, Kansas.

Many towns were founded by gold miners or railroad builders. After a period of wildness they settled down. Churches and schools were built. Touring companies brought plays, musical shows and circuses to towns. These were enjoyed by pioneers as well as by townspeople.

Many towns had saloons, although in some areas drinking was forbidden. Gambling was popular, but the average pioneer had very little money to waste on card games and roulette. What he had he needed for equipment and supplies.

The "Golden Eagle Clothing House" in Wichita, Kansas, in 1878.

RELIGION

When the West was first settled there were no churches. Pioneers worshiped at home. Sometimes neighbors took turns holding religious services. A stable, a barn or even the shade of a leafy tree was used as a place of worship. Once a town began to take shape, however, plans were soon made for a church to be built.

Some pioneer families took religion very seriously but others were not interested at all. Perhaps they felt they had more important things to do. To remedy this, traveling preachers visited the pioneers, often covering huge distances. They were nearly always made welcome by the isolated pioneers. The preacher would often stay overnight, and help the family with their chores. Sometimes other families would hear of his arrival and come to hear him preach.

Opposite *This pioneer church in Moro, Oregon, is still standing.*

Below *Visiting preachers sometimes called on the lonely pioneers.*

One of the most religious groups of settlers in the West were the Mormons. They are a Christian sect founded in New York State by Joseph Smith in 1830. He and his followers had to move westward because their beliefs made them unpopular. Smith was killed in 1843, but another leader, Brigham Young, took over and led them to Utah's Great Salt Lake. Here they built Salt Lake City. People came from other parts of America, Britain and Europe to join the Mormons.

Above *A Mormon wagon train heading for Salt Lake City.*

Recreation

Pioneers were usually so busy working that recreation was a luxury for them. But they did occasionally find time to stop work and enjoy themselves. The most popular sport was racing – on horseback, on foot and, by the 1880s, on bicycle. Many towns soon had their own race tracks. When they could afford it pioneers enjoyed gambling. If money was short they could bet their clothes.

Baseball and croquet were popular with westerners. Indoor entertainment included card games, like poker, dominoes and reading. Saloons were gambling and drinking centers. There were also billiard saloons and bowling alleys.

All westerners loved to dance, though sometimes, especially on ranches, there was a shortage of girls. The problem was solved by some men having to take the female part. There was also a shortage of musicians. Anyone who could play the fiddle could make a lot of money.

Weddings were a good excuse for everyone to have a good time, but the most important regular celebration was July 4th, America's Independence Day. Pioneers came from far and wide to eat, drink, dance, meet old friends and make new ones. At some stage in the festivities the Declaration of Independence might be read. This dates back to 1776 and marks the independence of the American colonies from Britian. At the end of the celebration, the pioneers would say goodbye to friends they might not see for another year.

A wedding photograph of two Kansas pioneers.

Opposite *July 4th, America's Independence Day, was always a cause for celebration.*

CRIME AND PUNISHMENT

Most western crime was committed by gangs of robbers and individual badmen. Pioneers were more concerned with trying to survive and make a living. However, some pioneers and cowboys took to crime as an easier and more exciting way of making a living. The West was so vast that criminals were able to hide out. Most, though, were finally either shot, hanged or imprisoned.

Pioneers were quite prepared to challenge badmen. A classic example happened at Northfield, Minnesota

Pioneers sometimes took to crime as a way of making easy money, but they were nearly always caught.

in 1876. The James Younger gang of train and bank robbers, led by Jesse James, tried to rob the town's First National Bank. The local citizens got together to protect their money and almost destroyed the gang with a hail of bullets.

Lawmen raised a posse, a group of citizens, to track down criminals. There were also vigilantes, men who took the law into their own hands. They often hanged their victims without a fair trial. The crime most usually dealt with by vigilantes was horse stealing. There were prisons and courts in the West but this form of instant justice too often took the place of a trial before a judge and jury. By 1900 the West was a more settled and civilized place. Crime had become more widespread in the cities.

A group of vigilantes, men who took the law into their own hands.

The End of the Frontier

In 1869 America was spanned by rail when lines heading east and west were joined at Promontory Point, Utah. This link, and later lines, made it possible for new settlers to be brought west far more quickly. In 1892 the United States Government announced that no more fertile land was available for settlers.

By the end of the century, pioneers and ranchers had settled most of their differences. Towns grew and more were built. Sodbusters were healthier as more doctors came West. Windmills were built to pump water from wells and new machinery and steel plows made farming easier. The West had been tamed but older pioneers did not forget the days when they had endured great hardships. They were the true makers of the American West.

By the turn of this century, the West had been tamed. This is the town of Pueblo, Colorado in 1910.

GLOSSARY

American Civil War Conflict which broke out between the northern and southern states of America in 1861 because the people of the south wanted to run their own affairs, which included the right to own slaves. The north won in 1865.

Bedbugs Small blood-sucking insects.

Cattle baron A wealthy rancher.

Indians The natives of America.

Molasses A syrup produced when making sugar.

"Quack" doctor A person who knows little about medicine but sells "miracle cures."

Roulette A gambling game in which a small ball is dropped onto a revolving wheel with numbered slots in it. People gamble on which slot the ball will end up in.

Sassafras tea A beverage made from the dried root bark of the sassafras tree.

Sect A religious group.

Trapper Someone who catches and kills animals for their skins.

Picture acknowledgments
The pictures in this book were supplied by the following: BBC Hulton Picture Library (The Bettmann Archive Inc.) 9 (right), 13 (bottom), 24, 30; The Kansas State Historical Society (Robin May Collection) 23 (both); The Nebraska State Historical Society (Robin May Collection) 11; The Office of the Secretary of the Interior (Robin May Collection) 19 (bottom); Robin May Collection 29; Peter Newark's Western Americana 6 (top), 7, 9 (left), 15, 19 (top), 27; U.S. Signal Corps (Robin May Collection) 11 (top); U.S. War Department General Staff (Robin May Collection) 26; Work Projects Administration (Robin May Collection) 6 (bottom).

INDEX

Baseball 27
Buffalo 10, 15

California Trail 5, 7
Children 10, 12, 13, 17, 19
Civil War (American) 15, 31
Clothes 12-13
Cowboys 23
Crime and punishment 28–29
Crops 10
Croquet 27

Dancing 27
Dangers 17, 20–21
Disease 17, 21
Doctors 16–17
Dugouts 8, 9

Entertainment 23, 27

Family life 10–11
Farming 10, 21
Food and drink 15

Gambling 23, 27
Godey's Lady's Book 13
Gold miners 23
Great American Desert 4, 5
Gunfights 23

Health and sickness 16–17
Homes 8–9
Horse racing 27
Hunting 15

Independence Day 26, 27
Independence, Missouri 4, 5
Indians 4, 7, 13, 15, 20, 31

James, Jesse 29
Justice 29

Law and order 23, 28–29
Locusts 21
Log cabins 6, 7

Mormons 25

Oregon 4
Oregon Trail 5, 7

Prairie schooners 6
Preachers 24–25

Railroads 23, 30
Range wars 21
Recreation *see* Entertainment
Religion 23, 24–25

Saloons 23, 27
Salt Lake City 25
Schools 18–19
Smith, Joseph 25
Snakes 16–17
Sodbusters 8, 9

Towns 11, 22, 23

Vigilantes 29

Wagons 4, 6–7, 25
Weddings 27
Women 10–11, 13

MURRAY AVE. LIBRARY
LOWER MORELAND SCH. DIST.
HUNTINGDON VLY., PA.